Make Yourself Marketable

I would like to thank Gerry Gottlieb for his suggestion to write this book and his advice, encouragement and persistence during the writing and production of the book. I would also like to thank Christine Berglind and Christina Gurry who formed the design team at Rapport Associates Ltd. for their hard work and dedication while designing and laying out this book. Special thanks, also, to my loving wife, Suzanne and my daughter, Laura Spoto for all their help and encouragement. Finally, thanks to my good friends Diane Ortiz and Debra Randazzo for their editorial assistance. Their contributions made this publication a better book than it would have been without them.

Table of Contents

Introduction
Make Yourself Marketable

At any given time, hundreds of thousands of people are searching for gainful employment. Are they searching for the right job for them? Are they chasing their bliss or are they only considering the limited options they've seen in newspaper want-ads? Do they even know what their bliss is? And if they do, are they searching in a way that will yield results? Once all of this is identified, is the candidate presenting himself/herself in the best light possible?

This book is intended to cover many aspects of career counseling finding the most viable career and employment path, writing resumes that work, questions to ask (and not to ask), the art of networking, how to deal with interviews and how to best market yourself in today's world. We'll also touch on how to deal with the age and gender factors, the right way to discuss compensation, changing careers, and the essential follow-up.

Chapter One
Choosing Your Career Path

Imagine waving a magic wand and having time to do whatever makes you feel happy and fulfilled. What would that be? Take some time to sit quietly and really think about it. Make a list of at least five things that you truly enjoy.

It is important not to limit your focus to just business related items. Be all inclusive. This basic approach is appropriate for the soon-to-be high school graduate, the long-time homemaker re-entering the workplace, a retiree who now has a little more freedom to enjoy and explore the next chapter of life, or the currently employed who may be finding their job to be a virtual prison sentence they must go to every morning. As important as the partner you choose in life, is choosing a livelihood that will allow you to live a life you will love.

Take the time to fully explore this first step. After all, you are now laying the foundation for the rest of your life. All the steps that follow will build upon this basic groundwork of knowing who you really are, what you enjoy and where you will be the most successful. There are many career personality tests to help you further define who and what you are: The Jung Career Indicator, The Meyers-Briggs Personality Test, MAPP (Motivational Appraisal of Personality Potential), The Keirsey Temperament Sorter, etc. You can easily find these on the web. Another great resource is your local bookstore. Books such as: <u>Career Match – Connecting Who You Are With What You'll Love to Do</u>

by Shoya Zichy, <u>The Pathfinder – How to Choose or Change Your Career for a Lifetime of Satisfaction and Success</u> by Nicholas Lore, <u>Do What You Are</u> by Paul D. Tieger & Barbara Barron, and, of course, <u>What Color is Your Parachute?</u> by Richard N. Bolles will take you through the critical steps essential to drawing the road map of your life and getting you focused and headed in the right direction unique to you.

Once you begin identifying the things you enjoy doing most – the things that give you personal pleasure and satisfaction, meet with a career counselor. You can explore the appropriate career paths that allow you to combine your personality, likes and comfort zones with your field of employment.

For example, a candidate was employed as the Senior Vice President of Marketing in a firm which provides consulting services to a broad spectrum of businesses. The working environment was unpleasant, at best, and the turnover of personnel was frequent as a result.

After some counseling, exercises and exploration, we began evaluating the possibility of a complete career change. One of the professions targeted by this client was teaching, in fact, his wife was a teacher. To paraphrase Lao Tze, he "decided to let go of what he was and become what he might be" – a teacher.

The first step was becoming involved at local universities and giving guest lectures. With a new focus, and a plan in place, he completed his PhD degree and is enjoying a new life as a college professor teaching, you guessed it, marketing!

Being happy, really enjoying life, having time for family and a rewarding career can all be your "lifestyle". Wouldn't it be great if your profession involved doing what you enjoy doing most in your personal life as well? Imagine the benefits.

If you are happy doing what you do, you will, most likely perform better at it.

Other things to consider:

• THE FAMILY BUSINESS SCENARIO
Your career path has been set at birth. Family responsibilities weigh heavily when one is virtually mandated to continue carrying on family tradition. Is there some way to modify what you do for the business that would be more in keeping with who you are and might better utilize your talents thereby upping your happiness?

• EDUCATION
The cost and time factor may also put limits on your desire for a particular career path. The legal field, accounting, engineering, health care, all hinge on specific educational credentials. Is there a way to play a supportive role in these fields if factors such as finances

don't allow a full degree in these specialized fields at this time?

• PERSONAL GOALS AND VALUES

Is being able to spend more time with family vital to your happiness? Is money the most important consideration? What about power, recognition, perceived social status, being a member of the "right" kind of country club, wearing the most expensive clothes, driving that fancy car?

• HELPING OTHERS

Does helping others play a key role in your life? Working for legitimate not-for-profit organizations; helping those in need as a profession, children, the poor and jobless, animals, protecting the environment? How important in your life is feeling that every day your efforts make your little corner of the world a better place to live?

• PUTTING IT ALL TOGETHER/LONGEVITY

Let's say you are an avid boater or perhaps even a professional competitive sailor. Obviously, age and physical capability come into play. What happens when your "time is up"? You can no longer physically be a professional sailor and be competitive, but your life and your bliss is sailing. What can you do to remain happy in your work and gainfully employed?

Imagine yourself dropping a pebble into the still water of a pond. Watch the ripples slowly move away from the center and expand outward. The expanding ripples represent potential avenues to explore and stay involved with your love of sailing. Each ripple is a person, sailing-related business, supplier of sailing products, a peer in the industry, a competitor, etc.

The list is almost endless and valuable if you maintain a history of credibility and a solid reputation. Use your contacts. Remember never to burn your bridges behind you even if the urge is there. Such action could come back to haunt you and we want to keep those ripples flowing and expanding!

Chapter Two
The Importance of Education

For decades, the significance of education and how it affects your life and career has been a popular topic of discussion and debate.

Does everyone need a college degree and graduate school?

Not so long ago, having a high school diploma was sufficient enough to land a corporate or executive job. Then came the era when a college degree was a prerequisite to those same jobs. Now, many feel that the minimum requirement for medium or high level corporate and executive positions has been raised to include a graduate or Master's degree. Of course, there are exceptions to every rule. Bottom line – get as much education as you possibly can to make yourself as marketable and competitive as you can be.

What school is the "right" school for you?

Many prospective job seekers ask themselves whether they need to focus on certain colleges or graduate schools. Is it essential to have credentials from a prestigious educational institution? Can you be successful and not have graduated from an "Ivy League" or other highly acclaimed college or university?

The answers, as one might expect, fall into several different categories:

Yes and no. Some areas, such as sales, can produce substantial earnings even without a degree from a big name educational institution.

Maybe. Not everyone can be successful in sales and, overall, the more education you have, the higher your earnings will be.

Affordability. Some simply cannot afford to pay for higher education. Don't give up. Check out various sources for funding and scholarships. Overall, education pays.

Depends on the individual involved. Some simply may not be suited for higher education and may prefer working with their hands or developing their own business.

The market place. Market conditions change. In tough times, a good education will always give you a competitive edge.

Desired life style. What is most important in your life?

One's personal life objectives. Keep in mind, education gives a candidate, other things being equal, a lifetime advantage.

THE COMPETITIVE EDGE

In most situations, having a solid educational background can make a significant difference. You may be more likely to get hired and recruited for job opportunities, including those with higher compensation.

In many instances, coming from the so-called "right schools" can be a factor in whether or not you are hired. Some refer to this as the good old "boy's club". Its influence depends in part on the management of the firm and the inherent culture.

Is this cast in stone? Definitely not!

One can readily point to many successful individuals who may not have even graduated from high school, yet were able to develop a successful business.

There are many successful earners who may not have attended or graduated from a higher educational institution but learned how to sell, work hard and became "street fighters." They may have affiliated with companies providing valuable products that people either wanted or needed. In other words, what these employees lacked in formal education, they made up for in determination, hard work, etc. They overcame what would be thought of as a limitation and become an integral and indispensable part of the company. Think about it for a moment. If business is off is the executive manager going to try to cut costs by getting rid of the producers the people who bring in the business – or will he/she find other areas to cut?

As a job seeker who lacks a degree from the "right school" or a Master's degree, you may be required to prove yourself – work your way up, so to speak. There are those that tend to look down at sales as a profession, but this is a mistake. Sales is often one of the fastest ways to grow in a firm, and effective sales people frequently become top earners and build their own following. They cultivate a customer base who appreciate good, honest service, prompt delivery and quick response should something go wrong.

Look even deeper and you will realize that, in essence, every employee is involved with sales either directly or indirectly – including the president of the company.

What is the best form of education?

Experts have differing opinions on what is the best form of education. There are a variety of scenarios that play an important role, but each person's needs are different and a review from a practical point of view is often the best route to take.

Let's look at the basics. A Liberal Arts track teaches you how to think and how to write. It can provide a platform on which to develop a career with a broad enough base able to survive unexpected fluctuations in the economy and business world. This, combined with additional advanced education, can prepare you by providing a choice of avenues to follow. It can help address changes in the employment marketplace that have become more the norm than the exception.

Specialized education, concentrates on a specific industry or narrowly focused area of expertise. This may involve specific disciplines such as data processing, engineering, design, research, etc. This can work fine in a status quo environment where the demand for certain skills remains constant; however, electing to focus on one area carries risk. It may be a "hot" field at the moment, but there are no guarantees. If the demand for that skill set dwindles, your specialized education approach could leave you less qualified to find another position that requires a different or broader range of skills.

The employment marketplace is constantly changing. The big demand for expertise in computers or data processing has slackened off – perhaps because of the "outsourcing" of jobs to foreign countries and the fact most people have their own data computers, allowing them to take care of much of their own data processing. The overnight success of the internet or "dot com" businesses have flattened out or, in many cases, evaporated and many of those companies simply disappeared. There is growth in Occupational Outlook Handbook, we'll see a tremendous amount of growth in service-producing industries. Some of the "hot" industries of the moment and on the rise involve health care (i.e. personal and home health aides, medical assistants, dental hygienists and assistants), professional and business services, automotive repair, leisure and hospitality, insurance, waste management, aerospace, engineering and related industries.

The combination of a solid liberal arts background, involving the basics of how to think, write and communicate, remain important and viable. This format often reflects on historical events and the impact they had on the marketplace. In the eyes of many, an advanced education is necessary to qualify for positions involving a broader spectrum of skills which may well be applicable to multiple industries.

The attitude of an employer plays a significant role in hiring. Some firms have a tunnel-vision philosophy. Who says that someone who markets red trucks would have problems marketing blue cars? Can we assume that an athlete who plays right tackle would not have the skills to also be suitable to play some other position?

Some firms feel that in order to be successful in their operation you have to have graduated from certain schools to fit in. Others tend to focus more on your accomplishments and overall track record.

In the multi-stage development of your career path, be aware of the factors mentioned here and try to investigate the climate of the company through the internet and contacts you may have, before you apply/interview. A heads up to the thinking of the people with hiring power will help you to decide whether or not to apply and to navigate an interview more successfully.

Chapter Three
The Art of Changing Careers

In life, we are often faced with deciding the necessity and the viability of a career change. Many different circumstances can play an important role in the decision process and it is very important to recognize and deal with them.

Consider some of the following scenarios:

You lost your job.

Your company was faced with having to lay people off and you happen to be one of the unfortunate employees being terminated. This may or may not relate to whether the business is no longer viable, the demand for the products or services is no longer there, the company is relocating, etc. Your company may have been sold and new management is bringing in their own people. The end result, however, is that you are out of a job, and not by choice.

Note: It is important to realize that reacting to a termination of employment is quite different from deciding to change jobs or careers while still employed without a firm, written commitment for your next job.

Loss of a job, the thought of having to relocate, change careers, etc. often contribute to added stress and even depression.

Stop! Take a deep breath, a short break, collect your thoughts and make every effort to think positively. In fact the whole situation, bad as it may appear at first glance, could be an opportunity for you to regroup. Remember the words of Ivy Baker Priest who said, "The world is round and the place which may seem like the end, may also be the beginning."

Negativity can adversely affect the overall situation, including how others, – possibly potential employers – see you. This is the time and the opportunity to get back to basics and rediscover what is most important in your life.

Develop that ideal list of what you enjoy doing. Speak to family, mentors, peers, friends regarding your thought process

Be positive and pro-active and do some research.

You may not fall in love with every suggestion, but try to keep an open mind.

Don't panic. This can show up in the job seeking process, blow interviews, etc. Try to stay cool and plan. Seek professional advice before muddying the waters.

There are many areas one can look for jobs. Networking with friends, ads, online, recruiting firms, etc. Think carefully before sending your resume to the entire world. That could have an adverse effect. When writing a resume, be honest. Being let go in today's times does not necessarily have the same degree of negativity as in previous years. If the company is cutting back, lacks business, this is understandable.

Severance packages can be extremely important. Generally firms offer one week's compensation for each year employed. This can vary, of course. Speak with your accountant. If you feel you were unjustly discriminated against, IE age, younger person brought in at lower salary, etc., consult with your attorney but don't rush to make an enemy. This can come back to bite you in the proverbial butt. Always try to leave in a professional manner. Your "current" employer could hire you back when things change or, if mishandled can hurt your chances of other employment when asked to provide a reference. Always a good idea to ask the company letting you go for written references.

You've decided to change jobs by choice.

Weigh your options carefully. Don't rush. If you are positive of the move, have everything in writing from your new employer. Say nothing bad about the company or people you are leaving and always provide proper notice, at least two weeks, before leaving. Your new employer should appreciate that you are a quality person and would treat his/her firm with the same professional courtesy. You may, however, be asked to leave immediately. Always leave on the best terms!

You've had a long hiatus from the workplace and are trying to get "back to business".

Be honest. Parenting, dealing with personal problems, injury, illness are part of life. Try to show activity during your hiatus. This could include charitable work, armed service for your country, etc. Emphasize skills, accomplishments and desire to get back to work and help your new employer add to their bottom line.

Chapter Four

How Best to Market Yourself

STEP 1: TO START

The first step is to be realistic in your approach. You need to think of yourself as a marketable commodity which is defined as the "Summation of your ability, education, experience and track record to produce a profit". Some people initially take exception and even offense to this approach as being impersonal and not addressing the fact that they are real people – human beings – not merely a commodity in the marketplace.

My response to these sensitive folks is to get real and acknowledge that to employers, it's all about the bottom line and who can get them there.

Thankfully, there are many firms that truly care about their employees as people and treat them accordingly. That is a desirable workplace indeed. To be employed by these companies, you must first receive an offer. You must emphasize your background of productivity and all that you bring to the table in order to get it. The luxury of simply hiring "nice" people doesn't address the need for companies to show bottom line profitability to remain competitive, grow and survive. The need for proven producers regardless of the position, is essential to thrive in this economy.

STEP 2: DEVELOP A MARKETING STRATEGY THAT WORKS

In this stage, one needs to structure a formalized strategy. Develop a marketing plan to present – the product – to companies illustrating why they need you to help increase their bottom line. Your first task is to prepare a detailed target list that should encompass the following considerations:

A. *Companies that are or have been your competitors* – Even if you may not view this avenue as your foremost choice, don't rule it out. At least, put yourself in the position of having options presented to you.

B. *Suppliers* – You may have established good relationships and your suppliers may appreciate your knowledge of the market and the value of your contacts.

C. *Customers/Clients* – The same value could be an added plus as stated under suppliers.

D. *Superiors, peers, subordinates* – You never know who can be helpful unless you explore. Conversely, you never know who might actually hurt you and hinder your progress. There are ways, "tricks of the trade" to test this out which we will discuss furthur on.

If you have created solid relationships, seeking personal contacts as referrals, etc. can be a viable approach. It depends on the situation and the degree of confidentiality needed.

Develop your personalized target list.

Prepare additional listings of companies that you may have an interest in joining, especially those that would benefit from what you bring to the table. Begin with those where you have direct experience. Include in your list, other firms where you have a strong interest in exploring, such as growth areas and companies where you may have contacts. For those just starting their careers, internships in your field of interest can help.

Turn to professional organizations/executive search firms that work in your areas of interest. Include organizations structured to assist in finding jobs and providing networking opportunities.

STEP 3: PACKAGING THE "PRODUCT"... YOU!

It is very important to note that there is no such thing as a single resume in today's market place. In a highly competitive market you need to have a resume tailor-made for each position you seek. The era in which one resume with a brief, bland, impersonal cover letter was sent out en masse is over. It is essential to have your resume stand out above all others. This subject will be covered, in depth, in Chapter Five.

STEP 4: THE ART OF NETWORKING

Networking, when done properly can be an extremely valuable tool. Friends, former peers and other business contacts, if carefully approached and not burdened by repeat calls, can be very helpful.

Prepare a list of anyone you think could possibly be of help – friends, neighbors, personal business contacts (especially, those employed or having connections with your target firms), former classmates, alumni relations and career development departments from schools you've attended, etc. In a comfortable setting you can test the waters. "John... confidentially I was considering changing jobs, one of the companies I had in mind was XX. I value your opinion, your thoughts? Do you know anyone there I can speak to? I'd appreciate any help you can give."

STEP 5: THE ART OF INTERVIEWING

An interview is what you have been looking for, so what is the best approach?

Be prepared. Conduct thorough research on the company. Find out who you will be seeing, their position, background data where possible.

Dress in proper business attire. Men, no earrings. Make sure your hair is properly cut. Obviously, ladies should also adhere to being dressed in a suitable professional manner. No overly tight or sheer clothing should be worn and no cleavage please! Keep jewelry and makeup minimal. Less is more.

Arrive on time. If concerned as to location, do a test run the day before and mark the route. Do not arrive too early and appear to be overly anxious.

When greeted by the interviewer, lean slightly forward, shake hands in a courteous manner. Don't squeeze too hard. Maintain eye contact and address the interviewer by name using Mr., Ms., or Mrs. whichever is appropriate. Thank them for taking the time to meet with you. When entering the office or interview room, wait to be seated by the interviewer. Maintain good posture and place your hands in your lap. Be yourself.

Be a good listener. Learn. Be prepared to answer questions such as:

Question: "Well, – tell me about yourself".

Response: Answer concisely. "I am married, have two children, earned my educational degrees from XXX and XXX. I was fortunate enough to be employed by XU and XU and received several promotions. I enjoy being active in the community (IE Rotary, little league, etc.)"

Question: "What prompted you to look at our company? What do you know about us?"

Response: "I'm glad you asked – many things. During my research, I learned that you successfully developed X and Y; (Name Company) has a rich background and compares favorably among other firms in your field like XXX (Name

Companies). Equally important, I have spoken to friends who work here or deal with your company and the comments were most favorable such as growth opportunities, how people are treated, etc.

Question: "What do you think you can do for us?"

Response: "I feel confident that I can add to your bottom line profitability. In my resume, I identify where I have been a consistent producer resulting in growth."

Question: "Why did you leave (or) what made you decide to leave your last position?"

Response: (Depending on situation) "The company has suffered severe losses in the current market place and this resulted in having to make extensive cut backs."

or

Response: (Leaving by choice) "I have enjoyed my association with XYZ company, however I don't feel that I am being fully challenged and the growth opportunities are slow in opening up. The compensation in many areas is not really competitive to similar firms."

Questions to ask:

Question: "What are the key areas that an appropriate candidate would be able to make a positive contribution to

(Name Company)?"

Question: "Do you have specifics as to what kind of ideal background a candidate should have that would most likely make him/her an asset to you?"

Question: "Why is the position available?"

Question: "What are the growth opportunities?"

Questions not to ask until a sincere mutual interest has been established:

Question: "Vacations, compensation, benefits, etc."

STEP 6: FOLLOW UP YOUR INTERVIEW.

Send a personal written letter to the individual who interviewed you. Use quality stationary, mark envelope "Personal and Confidential", and send the letter priority mail to glean attention. Express your appreciation for the time he/she spent with you. Indicate your sincere interest and enthusiasm in pursuing the opportunity. Indicate clearly, your interest in continuing the dialogue.

After one week if you have not heard back, make a personal phone call, preferably early in the morning, giving you a better opportunity to connect. Indicate your ongoing interest and ask if anything is required from you at this juncture.

STEP 7: USING REFERENCES

Supply references when asked. Select your references carefully. Use individuals who can honestly attest to the quality of your work.

Don't overuse the same reference. As time goes by, if the same person is called again and again, he/she will begin to wonder what the reason is that you can't seem to find a job. This could have an effect on the recommendation that they give of you.

If you suspect that the person you chose as your reference is not helping your job search or is, in fact, hindering your placement, you may want to have someone you know and trust call the individual in question and act as a potential future employer. Include questions such as: "Would you hire this person if you had an appropriate opening? Why did the individual leave? What was your relationship to the candidate?"

Chapter Five
How to Write Resumes That Work

Question: What is the main purpose of a resume?

The Average Response: To tell people about my background.

My Response: Fine, why not post it in the subway or on a bus and let everyone look and read about your background.

The Average Response: To let people know about my people skills, dedication, writing ability, how organized I am, my leadership abilities, etc.

My Response: Everyone claims all of the above, to the point that it is almost considered a "given." These claims take up meaningful space that can be better utilized.

The Average Response: To get the word out that I am available for hire.

My Response: Simply broadcasting your availability to the world often ends up in duplication where companies may receive multiple copies of your resume, whether sent by you, or agencies. Not only does this make you appear unfocused but less desirable. Letting people know you are available is simply not enough. The real purpose of a resume is to get you in front of the hiring authority.

If your resume fails to accomplish this key objective, it's not working effectively for you.

Have you ever been in the position of being the hiring

authority – the person who determines whether or not to initiate the actual hire? Think, and be honest in your response. When reading through a number of resumes, how far down each average resume do you really take the time to read? Most people read between one third and one half of the first page and often stop there unless given solid points that warrant reading further.

What does that tell you when preparing a resume?

Get your licks in early! Don't waste space with a lot of the verbiage found in 95% of the resumes out there. Let's start at the top.

Include Basic Contact Information.

Name, address, telephone number(s) where you can be reached, e-mail address, Fax (optional) etc. Regarding the e-mail address, do NOT use a cutesy name like Bulldog or Blonde Bombshell. Set up a new address for this purpose.

BE PROFESSIONAL!

Every aspect of communication reflects directly on how you are perceived. The same applies to your answering machine or voice mail's outgoing message. Put yourself in the position of the hiring authority. Which would elicit more confidence and respect?

"Hey, Bobbie the stud here, you know the routine, wait for the beep... later."

or:

"You have reached —, please leave a detailed message, your telephone number and I will return your call as soon as possible. Thank you for calling and have a pleasant day."

"OBJECTIVE"

Remember the importance of getting key items listed early. Don't waste space especially on the first page of your resume.

If you are considering including a paragraph or two stating your "Objective" at the top of your resume, look at it this way. If the "Objective": cannot specifically help you, then it's taking up valuable space and, in fact, could actually work against you – in which case, leave it out.

If you do decide to use one, then consider this:

A candidate preparing his/her resume is currently employed as the National Sales Manager for a small jeans manufacturer. He/she is responding to an advertisement from the XYZ Company seeking a National Sales Manager. The candidate puts in his/her resume: *"Objective: To obtain a position as Vice President of Sales*

*in a large jeans manufacturing company to utilize my
experience and skills, etc."*

Who's doing the actual hiring at the company? The Vice
President of Sales. He/she takes a look at the resume and
could very well think, "Hmmm, this person wants my job".
In this case, the form of "Objective" used, hurt the candidate's
chances rather than helped. What would have been a
more appropriate "Objective" to use? Consider a better,
tailor-made approach:

*"Objective: To obtain a position in Sales Management
with a larger jeans manufacturing company to utilize my
XU years of experience in adding to the bottom line
profitability to benefit the company and to enhance
personal advancement by performance."*

You may want to customize even further by naming the
company specifically in your objective – just be vigilant
about changing it and getting the correct name with each
submission!

If you are unable to create an effective objective that will
serve you, it may be best to do away with it and expand
upon the use of "Professional Overview".

"PROFESSIONAL OVERVIEW"

Professional Overviews supply key information early in the

resume to create interest. It entices the decision maker to read further by providing a concise summary of your business/professional experience and should be tailored to each company. You may also use "Business Experience Overview" as a headline. Using "Work Experience" or "Job Experience" does not present you as professional. Remember, in today's market there is no such thing as one resume. To be really competitive, you should have a resume geared for virtually every position you are seeking.

Remember not to waste space using common, over-utilized adjectives at the expense of stating specific performance, accomplishments, and your contributions in adding to the profit picture. Companies want to know what you can bring to the table that will add to their bottom line profitability. Do not be humble. Remember to state in summary form, the value you (the summation of your track record) can bring to the table.

Equally important is to provide specifics under your employment data that factually support your overview statements.

Example:

"PROFESSIONAL OVERVIEW"

"Over XU years experience in ABC and XYZ industries successfully adding to bottom line profitability resulting in the growth of the corporate employer and personal advancement based on performance."

You may also want to reference specific companies in your overview if they may serve as a plus factor. Among those companies to list would be well-known names of respected firms especially in the area for which you are customizing your resume. You MUST include specific examples showing proof of your "Professional Overview" performance claims.

HOW BEST TO ORGANIZE AND PRESENT DETAILS OF EACH EMPLOYMENT

Keep in mind it is important to show consistent growth by performance and avoid appearing like a "hopper" jumping from one company to another too frequently. A number of professionals elect to trace a candidate's growth by starting chronologically from education and proceed from that point.

This approach can work, if properly executed, and it does allow the reader to follow a career path from its inception.

However, many hiring authorities may prefer to be able to quickly review a candidate's most recent employment and accomplishments first, to avoid having to read through material that they – right or wrong – perceive as being less significant.

The chronological approach allows the writer the ability to apply specific accomplishments to each period of employment as opposed to a lengthy list without specific connection to a given company.

If the person involved in making the hiring decision has to try to figure out where the list of accomplishments took place, they may, in some cases, question their validity.

HONESTY IS THE BEST POLICY

Always tell the truth. Misstatements have a way of catching up with you especially when a thorough background check is conducted.

The most frequent areas of misstatements made on resumes are: education, dates, compensation and accomplishments.

During an executive search engagement, our firm was required to find a Division President for a leading cosmetic company. Among the candidates, was an accomplished female executive with eighteen years experience in the area sought by the hiring firm. She stated, on her resume, that she had received her MBA degree from a particular leading university. The candidate, in fact, virtually had the job subject to an in-depth background check conducted by our firm on behalf of the corporate client.

We discovered a few minor items involving dates (months, not years) which were a little "off". When it came to verifying that the candidate did, in fact, receive her Master's Degree as claimed on her resume we were unable to confirm her ever having received the degree. To make matters even worse, she hadn't actually attended the university she stated on her resume at all!

This misinformation had been included on her resume for eighteen years and had never been discovered. We advised the client about our findings and her dishonesty lost her the job. Your motto should be: TELL THE TRUTH. In the case above, and other cases involving false information, a company could fire an employee at any time in the future, should they discover he or she lied on an application or resume.

Avoid the following:

Previously we mentioned the importance of avoiding the appearance of "Job Hopping". After each chronological subtitle you would then go into specific detail, however in the examples below we cover the headline only.

Here is a prime example of what not to do:

October 1, 2005 to present. Senior Vice President XYZ Corporation.

June 15, 2004-September 30, 2005 Vice President Sales XYZ Corporation.

January 4, 2004-June 14, 2004 National Sales Manager XYZ Corporation.

October 1, 2003-January 3, 2004 Regional Sales Manager XYZ Corporation

January 2, 2003-September 30, 2003. Sales Representative ABC Corporation.

August 1, 2002-December 30, 2002. Sales Trainee ABC Corporation.

What's Wrong with the Previous Approach?

Resumes are often glanced at or skimmed while the reader hunts for key items of interest. The approach used above could and often will give the impression that each time period of change and/or new title could indicate another change in employer. The result, you may appear to the reader of being a "Job Hopper" and the assumption that you may not be the best person to hire because based on your resume you could very likely stay for a short period of time and leave again.

A Better Way to Use Dates.

Consider presenting the chronological approach as follows:

October 1, 2003 - Present. XYZ Corporation. (Total years spent)

June 15, 2005 - Present. Senior Vice President. (Promotion)

June 15, 2004 - September 30, 2005. Vice President Sales. (Promotion)

January 4, 2004 - June 14, 2004. National Sales Manager. (Promotion)

October 1, 2003 - January 3, 2004. Regional Sales Manager. (Promotion)

August 1, 2002 - December 30, 2002.   ABC Corporation.
(Different employer and total time period employed)

October 1, 2002 - December 30, 2002. Sales Assistant. (Promotion)

August 1, 2002 - September 30, 2002.   Sales Trainee. (Initial position)

Using the above approach clearly outlines total time spent employed at each firm as well as demonstrating the lack of jumping from job to job and depicts a consistent pattern of growth and promotion.

The result of the above approach is factual and honest but avoids the appearance of a candidate having different employers (job hopping) when quickly scanning the resume.

And now, you begin your search. View this as an opportunity to make positive changes in the quality of your life. Approach finding your new job as a full-time job. Read extensively about the field you seek. Conduct yourself with confidence and move forward, open to all the possibilities that present themselves while learning from the ones that do not. Thomas Jefferson said, "I'm a great believer in luck, and I find that the harder I work, the more of it I have." Go out into the world, work hard and make your own luck!

Testimonials

Letters of Appreciation

Here, you'll find several testimonials. These testimonials include comments from clients, who referred the services of IMA Search, Inc. to others. These clients found success in their careers by consulting with IMA Executives.

Additionally, you'll find representative comments from letters of appreciation. These letters were sent by several clients who received benefits from Career Counseling and wanted to express their gratitude.

Access Direct Systems Inc
171 Madison Avenue Suite 1600
New York, NY 10016

To whom it may concern:

As an executive with Access Direct Systems Inc. I had the opportunity to use the services of Paul Steinberg of IMASearch Incorporated.

Prior to Access Direct my division was owned by Acxiom Corporation at which time I had the need to look for and hire executive level positions.

We retained IMASearch for these projects and I must say that the results have always been favorable. Paul always conducted himself in a professional manner and the expertise he brought to the table always enabled us to fill positions with the most capable candidates.

I have also recommended Paul and his company to prospective hires who were successful in receiving professional advice from resume creation to securing the position they were looking for.

It was a pleasure working with Paul.

Very truly yours,
Thomas Gurry
ACS/Officer

Rapport Associates, Ltd.
1055 Stewart Avenue, Suite 18
Bethpage, NY 11714

Dear Paul,

I have run my company for twenty-eight years. The one thing that I have learned in that time is that change is inevitable for executive-level people, especially in today's fast evolving business environment. Adjusting to it is a challenge that most executives will face at one time or another.

In the last few years I referred several executives to you who needed to consider how to best advance their careers because of changes in their respective industries. You provided the guidance and advice to each of them that helped them to achieve new careers with more fulfillment and better compensation.

It is reassuring to know that a professional like you is available to act as a consultant and guide should the need to consider changing career paths arise. I wholeheartedly recommend you anyone facing a career challenge.

Sincerely,
Peggi Pugh
President
Rapport Associates, Ltd.

Clear Horizon Group, Ltd.
775 Park Avenue
Huntington, NY 11743

To Whom it May Concern:

I have utilized the services of Paul D. Steinberg,
President/CEO of IMA Search, Inc. I have introduced Paul
and IMA Search to several of my clients.

This introduction has provided them salient advice with their
executive recruiting needs. In addition, my clients have benefited
from the expertise that IMA Search provides in delivering Career
counseling services to those that are changing Careers, Finding
a new job, etc. This included providing resumes that really work
for each position, how to go about deciding the best path to
follow, how to market myself, how to network, the art of
interviewing, what to ask, what not to ask, etc. ...

As a Certified Financial Planner and trusted advisor to
executives and corporations; I feel that my services have truly
been enhanced...when I introduce my clients to IMA Search, Inc.

Gary J. DeLorenzo, CFP, MSFS
Clear Horizon Group, Ltd.

Nussbaum Yates Berg Klein & Wolpow LLP
Certified Public Accountants
445 Broad Hollow Road, Suite 319
Melville, NY 11747

To whom it may concern:

As the senior partner in our accounting firm, clients often ask me for referrals when seeking outside help.

I have referred clients looking to fill personnel needs to Paul Steinberg, President of IMA Search, Inc., and the results have been truly outstanding. Paul's competence and professionalism in completing the assignments not only satisfied the clients, they thanked me for making the referrals.

Paul's years of experience coupled with extremely high ethical standards sets him and his firm apart from the ordinary recruiters. The same applies to the outstanding Career Counseling Services provided by Paul and his firm.

It's a pleasure to work with him.

Very truly yours,
Richard E. Nussbaum, CPA

UBS Financial Services, Inc.
323 Earle Ovington Blvd.
Mitchell Field, NY 11553
516 745 1893

To whom it may concern,

I am a Senior vice president and CFP with UBS Financial Services Inc., one of the largest Wealth Managers in the world.

I have recommended Paul Steinberg to clients looking for job placement or career changes. The satisfaction my clients have expressed have been extraordinary. Paul's advice has truly been life changing, his professionalism and experience sets him apart, from other recruiters.

It is a pleasure to recommend clients and friends to Paul and his company IMA Search.

Very Truly Yours,
Harvey R. Wolf
Senior Vice President

About the Author

Paul D. Steinberg, President, Chief Executive Officer and founder of IMA Search, Inc. has over thirty years experience in the executive search and career counseling profession.

He has successfully managed search engagements for presidents, senior level executives, directors and key middle to senior management positions worldwide, covering multiple industries and disciplines.

Mr. Steinberg pioneered the unique and cost effective "Talent Reserve Bank" (TRB) program, a new and effective solution helping corporations prepare for the sudden and unexpected loss of key employees and other succession planning problems.

Mr. Steinberg also conducts lectures for groups, corporations, educational institutions, private organizations and individuals.

Prior to founding IMA Search, Inc. Mr. Steinberg held key executive positions with Burlington Industries, Celanese Corporation and Consolidated Foods. He received his B.A. degree in history from Bates College and his M.B.A. in marketing from the Columbia Graduate School of Business. Mr. Steinberg is listed in "Who's Who" and is President of the Executive Network, an association of senior executives from multiple industries formed to provide high level networking for members. Visit us at www.ima-search.com.

Mr. Steinberg is active in Rotary and the United States Coast Guard Auxiliary. He is an accomplished pianist, an author for numerous publications and a lecturer for several organizations.

www.ingramcontent.com/pod-product-compliance
Lightning Source LLC
Chambersburg PA
CBHW021024180526
45163CB00005B/2110